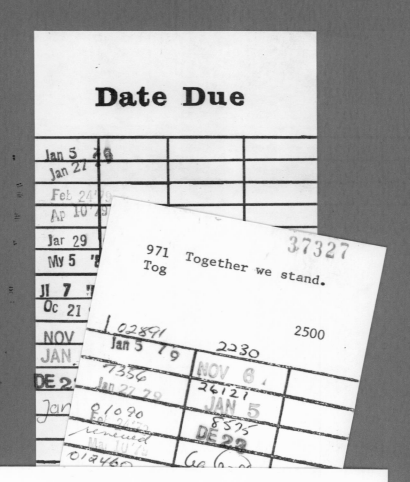

TOGETHER WE STAND

TOGETHER WE STAND

DONALD G. SWINBURNE

Gage Publishing
Toronto, Vancouver, Calgary, Montreal

Canadian Cataloguing in Publication Data

Main entry under title:

Together We Stand

ISBN 0-7715-9444-5

1. Canada. 2. Canada — Description and travel —
1950-   — Views.* I. Swinburne, Donald G.,
1949-

FC75.T64   971   C78-001363-8
F1016.T64

Design: Mario Carvajal

1 2 3 4 5 6 MMT 4 3 2 1 0 9

Printed and bound in Canada.

Acknowledgments

Without the unselfish help and counsel of the following people this project would not have been a reality:

J. Alex Houston
Gregory Keen
David Dick
Joan, Norma and Frank Swinburne
Bruce Wallace
Christopher Darling
Howard Mandel
Robert A. Barnett

A special thanks to John David Colombo for his kind permission to use many quotes from *Colombo's Canadian Quotations*.

The author and publisher wish to acknowledge their sources and thank the following parties for permission to reprint excerpts, as follows: Patrick Anderson, for use of a portion of "Poem On Canada"; a portion of "A Place: Fragments" from *The Circle Game*, 1966, by Margaret Atwood, published by House of Anansi Press Limited. Reprinted by permission; Edward Blake, "Aurora Speech," Aurora, Ontario; "east to west" from *Rocky Mountain Foot*, 1968, by George Bowering. Reprinted by permission of The Canadian Publishers, McClelland and Stewart, Limited, Toronto; *The Spectator*, July 6, 1901, for John Buchan's text; *The Toronto Star*, October 7, 1971, for Réal Caouette's text; Macmillan Company of Canada, Limited, for use of a passage from *Canada's First Century: 1867-1967* by Donald Creighton, 1970; Wm. Collins Sons & Co. Ltd., London, for use of a passage from *Grierson On Documentary*, edited by Forsyth Hardy, 1946; "Grain Elevator" from *The Collected Poems of A.M. Klein*, compiled by Miriam Waddington. Copyright©McGraw-Hill Ryerson Limited, 1974. Reprinted by permission; Tom Kneebone, for column written for "The Mermaid Inn," *The Globe and Mail*, May 20, 1978; a portion of "The Portage" from *The Shadow-Maker* by Gwendolyn MacEwen. Reprinted by permission of Macmillan Company of Canada, Limited, Toronto; a portion of *On Being Canadian*, 1948, by Vincent Massey. Reprinted by permission of J.M. Dent & Sons (Canada) Limited; the remarks of Louis St. Laurent, from an interview with Frank Rasky for *Liberty* magazine, 1958; Khushwant Singh, from "Oriental Pearl in the World Oyster," *Man And His World. The Noranda Lectures, Expo 67*, 1968; "The Lonely Land" from *The Classic Shades*. Reprinted by permission of The Canadian Publishers, McClelland and Stewart, Limited, Toronto; passage by William Toye, from the introduction to *A Book On Canada*, Wm. Collins Sons & Co. Canada Ltd., 1962; a passage by Pierre Trudeau, from *Wilderness Canada*, 1970, Clarke, Irwin & Company Limited.

For JOAN, FRANK and NORMA

MY COUNTRY

In the beginning, there was quietness for nothing grew or stirred on the land. Beauty abounded and yet the vastness sought out nourishment and companionship. And so, came the first trickles of life from the sky, and the rain occupied the lowlands and flourished in the form of a stream.

These first rains were pure and together the stream and the land prospered for many passings of the moon.

Hence, very gradually at first, all manner of water sought out this stream for it was a glorious place to be. Fallen rains gathered from far-off places and differing sources. Melted snow from the mountains married with the clear springs of the plains and together caused the stream to lengthen and open the gates onto the vastness. And soon the stream was great and powerful not only because of the land it flowed through but also due to the diversity of water that nurtured it.

As the years passed, the stream came of age and stature, notwithstanding the occasional drought or flood that only proved the water was sacred and worth preserving. The stream was clear and deep and its size caused a roaring that could be heard on many a far-off shore. For the stream was now a river and possessed a strength and character that was unmatched wherever rains fell.

But with size and depth, the river inherited obstacles that come with maturity. For in many places the currents had changed and certain portions sought to branch out and form tributaries.

And so, as time passed, inlets appeared in all the regions of the land, each seeking out new ways and surroundings. Yet, the river grew and became wiser, for it was sustained by rains from all manner of backgrounds and regions. But, as more time passed, the tributaries grew in strength and unwittingly entangled themselves in short-sighted opportunities to flourish. Some believed that the land they had carved and the uniqueness of the rains that emptied into their depths made them special — so special that they wished to dam up the water which had been their source for years and exist unto themselves. Other tributaries desired to align themselves with a different river, perhaps, to ease their own flow.

And in this troubled time, there came a flood of dissident rains that not only rejected the past but also sought to plot a new course for the future. Muddy waters spilled over the banks and onto the land, slowly washing away many of the glories which had made the land prosper. For the young waters were caught up in whirlpools of self-interest. And so, it appeared inevitable that the river would either divide or be consumed by an adjacent body of water.

Miraculously, the tides changed and fresh rain, not unlike the original trickles so much cherished and long forgotten, cleansed and made clear the future course.

And this fresh rain carried a message to every part of the waterway and it was slowly understood and believed by all. The message was this: total beauty, wisdom and strength are created when divergent streams flow into each other, together sharing the land and its future.

DONALD G. SWINBURNE

I know there are some who feel a sense of embarrassment in expressing pride in their nation, perhaps because of the fear that they might be considered old-fashioned or parochial. I do not belong to that group. I realize that a warped and twisted nationalism is productive of tyranny. But a healthy loyalty and devotion to one's country constitutes a most fruitful inspiration in life.

HON. JOHN DIEFENBAKER
Prime Minister of Canada (1957-63), House of Commons, July 1st 1961

This country is without doubt a richer, greater country with Quebec a full partner. And this province and our citizens will work together to maintain a united Canada.

I would want to observe in the year 2000 some historian writing about Canada in terms of comparative economic contribution. No province will get even close to the billions of dollars contributed by Alberta between 1973 and a future date through agreeing to stage-in oil and gas prices for the benefit of all of Canada. So no Albertan should be defensive about this province's commitment to Confederation.

Clearly we are Canadian before we're Albertan.

PETER LOUGHEED
Premier of Alberta

Keep our people together in a land
where they can maintain their own
individuality.

ABBE ANTOINE LABELLE
Deputy Minister of Colonization for Quebec, 1888

I'm not sure for myself that I know what Canada is, and all regionalism, all particularism and, in the end, all nationalism worries me. I offer instead a line from James Baldwin: "The moment we cease to hold each other, the moment we break faith with one another, the sea engulfs us and the light goes out."

JUNE CALLWOOD
Journalist, T.V. Personality

The attitude of many people here and elsewhere across Canada to the threat of Quebec separatism is a resigned and very regrettable one — "Let them go!" I urge all of us, singly and together, to join in forcefully rejecting this attitude. I urge that we assess very carefully and accept the broad advantages of our Confederation as opposed to the disadvantages.

I have no doubt that we can come to a common conclusion that Confederation is indeed worth our efforts to preserve it.

The fact of the matter is that the vitality and viability of our Canadian Confederation is now at a crossroads. Because of the avowed intention of the new government of the province of Quebec to seek, by referendum, to bring about its independence, we are challenged to close ranks in a spirit of national understanding, coupled with determination that the existence of our country will be assured.

Put aside your apathy. In its place sharpen your sensitivity toward Canada. No country, least of all ours, will easily come apart if its people care enough. Hence, we must not only care, but we must seek to demonstrate our care, indeed our commitment. We have to become, "aware of the richness of our diversity." In so doing we must

remember and be proud that our diversity and our heritage are rooted in, and based upon, the toleration and the greatness of our two founding peoples.

I believe this country is worth saving.

JOHN J. VOLRICH
Mayor of Vancouver, British Columbia

I know the worth of this unprecedented idea, the idea of unity without uniformity which is the distinctive mark of Canada, the stamp of the Canadian identity. That is why, despite some present-day trends and fashions, I do not—I cannot imagine a Canada without Quebec, or a Quebec without Canada . . .

DUFF ROBLIN
Premier of Manitoba (1958-67)

As a child born in Canada to a young and vital immigrant couple, I was raised speaking one language in the home and another outside. Although this never did change completely, as the years went by and the family grew, the English language became the dominant tongue. This all seemed very natural and, although regret was occasionally expressed, the loss of the first language was accepted without very much of a struggle.

Because of this experience I can understand why families in this country who have used French at home for generations, would question the requirement to use English at work or elsewhere. Of course — associated with language are cultural activities and the history and heritage of the family and community.

Recognize this feeling and you see Canada as it really is. Ignore this and there will be no Canada.

SAMUEL DAVIS
Mayor of Saint John, New Brunswick

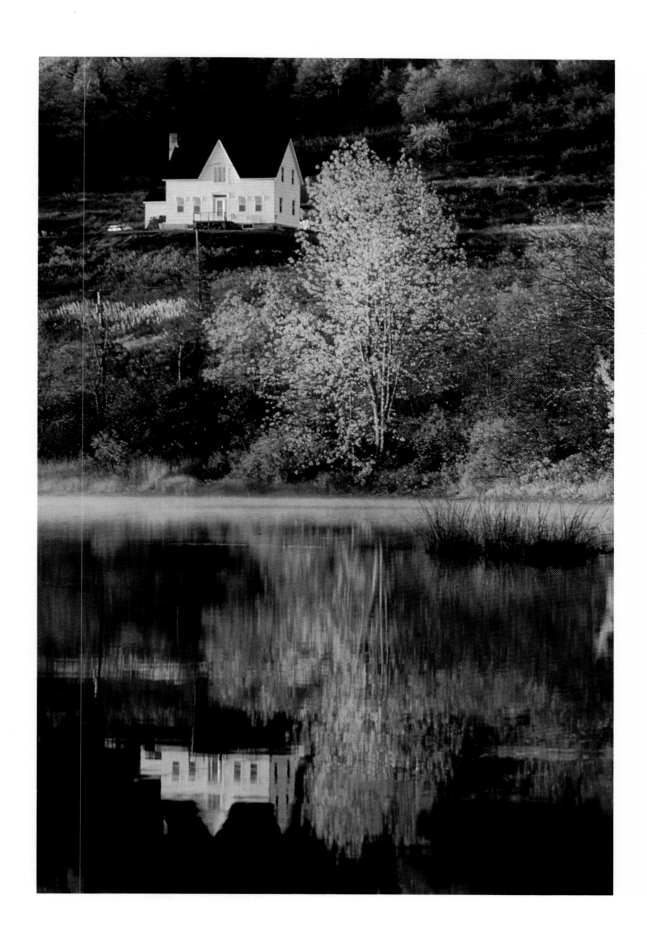

A little while and I will be gone from among you, whither I cannot tell. From nowhere we came, into nowhere we go. What is life? It is a flash of a firefly in the night. It is a breath of a buffalo in the winter time. It is as the little shadow that runs across the grass and loses itself in the sunset.

CROWFOOT (1830-1890)
Canadian Blackfoot Indian chief, April 25, 1890

I hope that in writing this article I am expressing the feelings of a great many Canadians—Canadians, like myself, who keep a home, do their work, have fun and talk back to the TV.

I am tired of what seems to be piecemeal presentations of our side of the Quebec vs. Canada situation—excerpts from radio talk shows, one-line statements from person-in-the-street interviews. There is nothing concrete or coherent—never an in-depth look at how we really feel. I wish I had a soapbox as big as Paul Bunyan's blue ox to express my views.

The Prime Minister refers to us as English Canada. To call us that is an insult to all the other nationalities that have settled here and make up our great Canadian mosiac. Even myself. Calling me an English Canadian is ignoring my ancestry. It includes Norwegian, Dutch, Cree, Scottish, English, probably Hungarian, and who knows what else? Aren't we all Canadians first—a new nationality? A new race of people in a young, new country.

I am a Canadian who speaks Canadian English, and anyone who doubts that statement should go over to England and hear the difference. Maybe the time will come when our language will be called Canadian. I was amused recently to read about a writer who was born in the United States, raised in England after he was seven years old, who returned to the United States to learn American so he could write in that style. As Rex Harrison said in *My Fair Lady* when talking about speaking English, "Why, in America they haven't used it for years."

The Prime Minister says we must understand the French of Quebec and make them feel at home in the rest of Canada. What about them making us feel at home in Quebec? I would gladly learn French if I knew my counterpart in Quebec was learning English. It's a two-way street. Why should we be encouraged to be bilingual while Quebec has Bill 101? That's what we resent! That kind of favoritism doesn't work in family life. How does the Prime Minister expect it to work in holding a nation together?

I give praise to the Ukranian-Canadians. They are keeping their language, cultures and customs alive in all art forms while adding to our Canadian way of life, not dividing it. Many others are doing the same.

I feel we who speak only one language are poorer because of it but the Canadians in Quebec who speak only French are poorer still. Think of all the places around the world that we can visit and feel at home in—even beautiful Hawaii!

Do I want to see Quebec separate? No! I realize that language isn't the only issue involved in separation talk. I was born and raised here in Saskatchewan and love travelling. I've enjoyed every place we have visited in Canada but I'm always glad to return home to Saskatchewan. I was a child of the thirties, so grew up feeling we (the province) were one of the poor relations in a large family (Canada) but we are still trying, taking our place and sitting down with the top representatives to iron out our differences.

If Quebec does separate what will it have gained? It will still be a minority: a small nation surrounded by two large nations.

Again I ask myself—do I want to see Quebec separate? No! So much of our history is entwined and I believe there are a great many in Quebec who want to stay a part of this great country. I sincerely pray this crisis is settled as peacefully and fairly as possible.

VELMA M. CAMPBELL
Homemaker, Melfort, Saskatchewan

I participated along with other "talk hosts" from across Canada in the Canadian Association of Broadcasters Trans-Canada telephone phone-in show that dealt with the future of this country. That experience convinced me that most Canadians, English and French-speaking, want to see this country stay together.

I said on that program that if any of my fellow Canadians feel they are carrying too many of the burdens of Confederation then they should take the time to visit the Maritimes and, in particular, the Cape Breton area. We too have had our share of problems within Confederation, but we also have our share of its beauty and strength. I would venture to say that no more than a very small fraction of us Maritime Canadians would want to see this great country split up in a political power play.

I'm confident that Canada will remain united from coast to coast and that all Canadians will work toward building a stronger Canada. The political ground rules may change, but Canada will survive.

NORRIS L. NATHANSON
Broadcaster, Sydney, Nova Scotia

32

Awake, my country, the hour is great
with change !
Under this gloom which yet obscures
the land,
From ice-blue strait and stern
Laurentian range
To where giant peaks our western
bounds command,
A deep voice stirs, vibrating in men's
ears ...
Awake my country, the hour of dreams
is done !
Doubt not, nor dread the greatness of
thy fate ...

SIR CHARLES G. D. ROBERTS
from "An Ode For The Canadian Confederacy"

… I have wandered over many lands in many climes and lived among diverse races … I remain as convinced as I was 20 years ago that there is no country in the world as beautiful as Canada, and there are no people in the world nicer than Canadians. To me, coming back to Canada is like coming back to my spiritual home. Canada quickened in me the impulse to appreciate the best there is in life; the ability to perceive beauty in things that are beautiful; the ability to love people who are lovable. It was in Canada that the desire to write came upon me … I owe more to this country and its people than I can put into words. Many among you will be embarrassed by this kind of soppy sentimentalism. Well, I am a soppy sentimentalist.

KHUSHWANT SINGH
Indian lecturer and author,
from Noranda lectures, given at Expo 67

Whatever you do adhere to the Union
   ... we are a great country and shall
become one of the greatest in the
universe if we preserve it; we shall sink
into insignificance and adversity if we
suffer it to be broken.

SIR JOHN A. MACDONALD
Prime Minister of Canada (1867-73, 1878-91), 1861

CPR—binding East to West
slab after slab laid down
thru Rocky Mountains
steel bent by will
and bending
till Vancouver
and steel-pushers left
along the track . . .

GEORGE BOWERING
from "east to west"

Most families experience conflict as children grow up and members grow apart, each following their chosen course in life. These conflicts do not normally destroy a family although they frequently add spice and sometimes bitterness to life. However, as a rule the family goes on and sometimes it is stronger over the years because of those conflicts and because nobody tried to pretend they didn't exist and paper them over.

So it is with a country. I know that we have conflicts and that we always have had conflicts, and I don't expect that situation to change. Nor do I see any reason why it should, human nature being what it is. I see no point in pretending that we don't have conflicts or in doing anything but pursuing our own chosen course and dealing with the conflicts as they come — just as we would do in our own families. This doesn't make for harmony but it certainly makes for a normal life in a normal country.

I cannot, therefore, endorse the many sincere efforts that are made today to bring people together in an atmosphere of sweetness and light. No such atmosphere can, in my view, achieve much of value. What is needed is a degree of maturity that permits us to have our quarrels without burning down the house and to accept each other's differences without trying to reconcile them or pretend that they don't exist.

It may be interesting that my family is French Canadian and French is the first language of some of my children. However I have lived and worked in the East and the West and I know Canada as a multi-racial country, a country which has welcomed immigrants from all over the world for hundreds of years. It is my firm belief that the majority of people in this country will not accept, and should not accept, any attempt on the part of the federal government to impose a bi-racial fiction on this multi-racial country. Concentration on our differences exacerbates conflict.

ROD SYKES
Mayor of Calgary, Alberta (1969-77)

The future of Canada, I believe, depends very largely upon the cultivation of a national spirit....We must find some common ground on which to unite, some common aspiration to be shared, and I think it can be found alone in the cultivation of that national spirit to which I have referred.

EDWARD BLAKE
Premier of Ontario (1871-72), October 3, 1873

Sometimes there's a tendency to evaluate our state of cultural and sociological well-being by comparing it with the rest of the world, but then we are overlooking the fact that Canada is unique — both in its characteristics as a nation and in the troubles which those characteristics produce. The country's many ethnic groups, its size and sparse population demand a creative, new approach.

For, just as Canada's problems aren't identifiable with any other nation's, neither are its solutions. For me, no identity crisis exists here. Part of the charm of this country comes from its ability to honor the integrity of its ethnic groups — rather than to demand their assimilation.

A true Canadian culture springs from being here, living here and benefiting by the free exchange of ideas across the land.

HAGOOD HARDY
Canadian composer and musician, Toronto

My feeling for the capital of Canada which I have come to love, began when I first saw it as a young soldier in World War II. But I can't help wondering what I would have felt, in visiting Parliament and the institutions of which I was so proud, if no one could speak my language. I'm sure that if I had found English treated, at best with tolerance, often with contempt, and always by exception, that I would have wondered what my place was in my country. I certainly would not have felt at home.

My regiment formed one of the three battalions of the Eighth Canadian Infantry Brigade under Brigadier Archambault, a much-decorated veteran of World War I.

Somehow we survived — though not all of us by a long shot. The gravestones in Normandy are tragic testimony to that. The brigade fought with distinction, and beside those tombstones carved with the names of four of my five closest friends are such names as Leblanc, Thibeault, Nadeau, Gougeon and Tessier.

After the war Quebec was still looking in on itself, dominated by often oppressive political regimes and sometimes medieval church structure. Elsewhere in Canada, French Canadians had to settle for second-class status and even in Quebec they had little hope of gaining access to the better jobs and opportunities Canada presented.

But a new generation was beginning to take over, men like Gérard Pelletier, Jean Marchand, Jean Lesage, René Lévesque, Claude Ryan, Maurice Sauvé, Maurice Lamontagne and Pierre Trudeau. These were leaders who would not tolerate the indignities of the past, men committed to Quebec and no less committed to Canada, and optimistic, or at least hopeful, that Canadians were big enough, far-sighted enough, sensitive, enlightened, and decent enough to make it all work. Skeptics on both sides failed to deter them, and they chose to go out and fight on three fronts: at home in Quebec, across the country, and in Ottawa.

Today, Quebec's French culture is one of the healthiest in the world. Radio Canada produces more live television in French than the national network of France. Seventy-five per cent of the films shown in schools in Quebec are French Canadian originals or versions. French Canadian film-makers like Claude Jutras, Denis Arcand and J.P. Lefebvre are known in the 27 countries that show their work. Theatre, ballet, opera, concert music, all are thriving, and Quebec *chansonniers* have for years been the toast of Paris. And all this is primarily due to the federal presence in Montreal of the CBC, the NFB, and the Canada Council.

In Ottawa, French and English have equal status throughout the government. Francophones, now 27 per cent of our population, make up 25 per cent of our public service. Their share of jobs is still too low in some categories — administrative and foreign service, technical, scientific and professional — but the catch-up rate for the past five years is striking: rising from 37 to 86 per cent. At the top, Francophones hold 20 per cent of executive positions and their present rate of increase should take them to parity in the early 80s without sacrificing the merit principle.

This transformation has taken place almost everywhere in government. In the House of Commons, for example, we now have a simultaneous translation system which ensures that both languages are equal. Bilingualism in the House of Commons is no longer theory, it's a fact.

We haven't done all this without some misunderstanding, a feeling that maybe the change has gone a little too far, too fast. But when the resentment has faded and we look back on this era, we may agree that the waste and mistakes were a necessary part of the cost of redressing a hundred years of injustice in a decade. Because this is what we have tried to do — and are doing — in Canada, so that young Québécois visiting Ottawa as I did so long ago, will see it as the symbol of their country and feel it as theirs.

MR. BARNEY DANSON
Minister of National Defence

Let us develop in our citizens a deep sense of Canadian loyalty and national pride.

Nature endowed us with a magnificent setting, our ancestors developed an impressive culture; let every man, woman and child use the democratic process to contribute, each according to his talent, to the creation of one Canada.

LORRY GREENBERG
Mayor of Ottawa, Ontario

52

A box: cement, hugeness, and
rightangles —
merely the sight of it leaning in my eyes
mixes up continents and makes a
montage
of inconsequent time and uncontiguous
space.

A.M. KLEIN
from "Grain Elevator"

Canada is a unique nation. The concept of Canada at its formation was that it would be a country based on union without conformity; this provides the distinctive cachet of the Canadian personality. And that is why Canadians of goodwill in all parts of the country, and in spite of current fashions and current moods, cannot envisage a Canada without Quebec or a Quebec without Canada. For if this were to happen, we would all be the losers, in the economic, the cultural and the historic sense.

Canada, like every other nation in the world, has its internal differences — mostly economic. There is no doubt that any section of Canada can claim it has been misused or abused by our economic and political structure. Quebec can rightly claim economic and cultural problems imposed by history and by certain operations of the federal system. The Maritimes, too, can claim real and serious problems in economic development and growth, as well as in energy. We in the West can parade a whole shopping list of grievances, partly economic, partly geographic.

We all have our problem areas, and we will argue with other provinces and particularly the federal government to try to get better terms for our province and our region. But it will be done within the Canadian context; we will not let impatience destroy our future.

We must work with every means at our disposal to keep united. The great Canadian experiment in political bi-nationalism and cultural plurality is working. We are proving that distinct cultures can flourish within the bosom of a single state, to their mutual advantage and growth. And as Canadians, whatever our mother tongue, what we must do now is to rediscover and to restore the hard-won fraternity that united us at Confederation and unites us now.

We can then show the world, and more importantly show ourselves, that we are one: we are Canadians.

EDWARD SCHREYER
Premier of Manitoba (1969-77)

The government of British Columbia is fully committed to the concept of a united Canada and to the basic principles of the Canadian federation—to the idea of Canada, one nation, from Atlantic to Pacific, comprised of five regions each with its own strengths and character, brought together by common bonds.

Ours is the third largest province in Canada in terms of size, population and most other indicators of importance. It encompasses 360 thousand, square miles making it larger than Washington, Oregon, California and the state of New York put together. Few may realize that Victoria, our most southerly city, is some 350 miles north of Toronto, and that Prince George, considered by some to be the north of the province, is closer to our southern boundary.

But diversity in geography, language, culture and economics among the various regions of Canada, can be one of our great strengths in nation building.

To one of the regions, preserving a culture and language is of paramount concern; to others, unequal economic opportunity is the greatest problem requiring redress; to still other regions, developing a sound and lasting industrial base is of prime importance. The strength of the nation lies in recognizing its diversity and meeting the challenges it brings.

These differences of geography, in resource potential and the varying mosaic of people have always called for a special sense of purpose—a will to make our country work. Canadians have consistently experienced some difficulties in nation building but to date we have risen to the occasion. I am confident that we will continue to do so. We ought not to be fearful that the future requires us to show flexibility in our constitutional arrangements, nor ought we to be fearful that the future requires us to make serious choices. Canada's future belongs to those who, with confidence, are ready and willing to accept the challenge of making such choices now. My government accepts the challenge and will continue to present creative yet realistic solutions toward a better and united Canada.

WILLIAM BENNETT
Premier of British Columbia

The problem of a separate Quebec had come to obsess and monopolize the minds of both English and French Canadians. It had distracted them from other and more vital tasks. It blinded them to the peril that threatened their existence as a separate nation in North America.

DONALD CREIGHTON
Canadian historian, from *Canada's First Century: 1867-1967*

Wherever we look in the world today, or however far back in history, we find that the great moments in the collective life of the citizenry are usually a summons to nation-building or to nation-saving. Today we in Canada are summoned to both. In this House and in every province of this country, we are fighting—fighting to preserve a great and precious country. The most effective weapon we have is understanding. Debates, task forces, language programs, constitutional proposals—all these will be to little avail unless we have the ability to summon understanding and generosity toward each other's aspirations as individuals, as members of cultural and regional communities—and as Canadians.

I know that the task for Canada will not be easy. But was it easy for the Canadians who settled this sometimes harsh land? Was it easy for the Fathers of Confederation? Or for the early explorers who penetrated to all corners of this unknown continent? No, the task of creating, and re-creating, Canada has never been easy. But now the task is ours; and the task shall be accomplished. After all, the odds were much greater against those earlier Canadians who built from scratch this unexpected and even unlikely nation; a nation which—politically, socially, economically—is now one of the freest and most advanced in the world. Where they built with their hands and their heads—"conquering" nature, devising vast transportation systems—we must now build with our hearts. We must now decide how we want to live together, and better govern ourselves —so that all our children may live in a Canada which is truly united, and truly itself.

PIERRE E. TRUDEAU
Prime Minister of Canada

I'm a one Canada man and I've always been a one Canada man. I say the same thing coast to coast. When I put my foot on the dog's tail in Halifax, it barks right in Vancouver.

REAL CAOUETTE M.P.
Former leader of Social Credit Party, October 7, 1971

There are some 2,500 languages and dialects on this earth. There are less than 150 states in which to accommodate them. Most of the countries of Africa and Asia are trying desperately to preserve unity and civilized behavior with linguistic and cultural divisions far worse than ours. Our challenge is not ours alone: it is the challenge of a diverse humanity crowded onto a small planet. Our two peoples in Canada are among the most fortunate in the world — in wealth, education, cultural enrichment and traditions of personal freedom. French philosophical humanism and British Parliamentary democracy are among the great accomplishments of civilized man. We are inheritors of both traditions in a way that is unique in the world. If we fail — after 110 years of free self-government as one country — who can hope to succeed in solving this basic problem of the human condition? Both our communities must find the greatness of spirit that will accommodate our two languages and our two cultures in mutual generosity and full equality so that Canada can and will endure.

GORDON ROBERTSON
Secretary to the Cabinet for Federal Provincial Relations

The West has many grievances against central Canada, and against the way federalism has been interpreted by successive federal governments. Saskatchewan in particular has been at the mercy of decisions made elsewhere in Canada, often without reference to the needs or desires of the people of Saskatchewan. In Saskatchewan we have no access to the sea. We are dependent for our economic life on a transportation system devised and controlled by the federal government, not necessarily in our interests. We ship wheat and minerals out of the province, and import manufactured goods, in the classic pattern of a colonial state.

In Saskatchewan we have often felt that the rest of Canada makes us sell our products at low prices and buy what we need at high prices. In other words, we have felt exploited. Much of the political history of Saskatchewan can be understood in terms of our desire to reduce this perceived exploitation in order to become masters in our own house.

Nevertheless, I think I speak for Saskatchewan when I reaffirm my faith in Canada. I do not want the western provinces to leave Canada. I do not want Quebec to leave Canada. Canada is one of the most remarkable experiments in the history of nations. It defies geographic logic. In the minds of some it defies cultural logic, and yet it has survived for more than a century.

In Saskatchewan our feeling for Canada goes far beyond profit and loss. We are the only province where a majority of the people are of neither French nor British origin. Except for our people of native origin, Saskatchewan people came to Canada; Canada did not come to them. They have no other strong loyalty. They have ethnic ties to other lands and other cultures, but their loyalty, their undivided loyalty, is to Canada.

In Saskatchewan our people are the children and grandchildren of people who chose Canada and who with all their soul said: "This is my own, my chosen land. I have accepted it and it has accepted me."

So the feeling for Canada is powerful. Our feeling is that all Canadians will be poorer socially and spiritually if Confederation is weakened.

While I can understand and sympathize with the desire of the people of Quebec for a greater degree of effective independence, I nevertheless strongly believe in Confederation. I do not view this as a contradiction. I view it as a challenge.

The challenge is to recognize the

various grievances, in Quebec, in the West, and elsewhere in Canada and to ask ourselves what price we are willing to pay to preserve Confederation.

As we try to answer that question, we should remember that what distinguishes the history of Canada is the spirit of compromise. Our two founding nations engaged briefly in armed conflict, but soon found a way to live and work together in a spirit of mutual tolerance and respect. We did not join in the American rebellion against Britain, but found a way to achieve our independence without bloodshed and without rejecting the values of our parent countries. When our ancestors found that the Act of Union of 1840 was not working, they did not fall into warring groups, but instead came together again and created the Confederation which has lasted to the present day. The Fathers of Confederation understood that Canada was unique in the world, and that for the country to survive, all regions and all classes would have to compromise. And they understood, too, that these compromises could not be forced.

The tradition of compromise to which I refer is not, as sometimes suggested, a craven tradition. Rather it is a noble tradition — very much worth preserving. And it is a tradition which provides the solution to our present dilemma.

Canada was born out of accommodation.

It will survive by accommodation.

ALLAN BLAKENEY
Premier of Saskatchewan

Canada is essentially a country of the larger air, where men can still face the old primeval forces of Nature and be braced into vigor, and withal so beautiful that it can readily inspire that romantic patriotism which is one of the most priceless assets of a people.

JOHN BUCHAN
Governor General of Canada (1935-40), July 6, 1901

72

...When I grew older, I thought of those
lakes as mirrors
in which Aunt Hildegarde had never
seen herself—
brisk pits to show her soul and
Canada's.
And, as a matter of fact, she often
declared
she'd visit them one day. But she never
did.
A cancer engrossed her, she grew thin
and died.
Her lawyers, they say, had a hell of a
time
trying to sell that marvelous empty
neck of the woods that no one had ever
seen.

And the land was. And the people did
not take it.

PATRICK ANDERSON
from "Poem on Canada"

74

Dear Canada,

When I was a teenager I had a desire to get to know you. It led me to Château Lake Louise where I ran an elevator and discovered that mountains change their colors every day and can hypnotize you. It also made me spend many long days paddling a canoe, past endless rows of trees in northern Ontario. I posed for postcards on perfect P.E.I. beaches and went to school in a village on the St. Lawrence. That was the summer of '49.

I don't remember anything about the classes. But the important things happened after school anyway. All the pretty English girls got French boyfriends. And the pretty French girls got English boys. We went around in a big gang and sang a lot.

There were a couple of problems. Any conversation concerning religion turned into an angry shouting match. Our adolescent solution was to simply ban all religious discussion.

And then there was the question of whose language to speak. Boys were mostly more aggressive than girls in those days. So most of the time, they learned and we taught. My summer love would speak French so rapidly that I would soon become exhausted by it, and let him go back to English.

My French wasn't good at the beginning of the summer, or at the end. But it was better than some people's, like the woman in my boarding house who taught French in an Ontario high school.

Then I stopped learning about you, Canada. Instead I did a great many other things. But in all those years I never did anything for you.

Now my life seems to have settled down, not yours. And I think the best thing I could do for you, and the thing I'd like to do anyway, is just start really seeing you again. I'd like to know you deep down, on my own street and everywhere.

You may not last forever. And I know I won't. But I'm so at home with you.

WENDY BUTLER
Radio Broadcaster, Toronto, Ontario

With two colonial beginnings, two
languages, two main religions, Canada
is really two countries, held together by
three nation-saving bywords ...
conservatism, caution and compromise.

WILLIAM TOYE
Editorial Director at Oxford University Press, 1962

Despite the barely restrained pessimism of the media (and others) when they discuss Canada's future, I firmly believe that a united Canada will prevail.

As Canadians we are intensely interested in our similarities and our differences, in the incredible beauty surrounding us, and in the idea of Canada and all that we have come to represent. Expressing this interest, we continue to buy hundreds of thousands of books covering every aspect of the Canadian experience — from pictorial books to historical treatises. I have seen literally hundreds of Canadian books sent as gifts, year after year, to every corner of the world.

I remember, when I was quite young, being fascinated by Alex Colville's painting "Horse and Train" — a dark, wrenching, scene of a horse galloping along a railroad track toward an oncoming train's bright beam, and seemingly hypnotized by the light. I believed then that the horse leapt off the track and saved itself; and I believe now that we, as Canadians, will do the same.

CHRISTOPHER KEEN
Bookseller, Toronto, Ontario

I didn't know at first that there were two languages in Canada. I just thought that there was one way to speak to my father and another to talk to my mother.

LOUIS ST. LAURENT
Prime Minister of Canada (1948-57)

I think we can claim that it is Canada
that shall fill the 20th century…
whenever my eyes shall close to the
light it is my wish—nay, it is my hope—
that they close upon a Canada united in
all its elements, united in every
particular, every element cherishing the
tradition of its past, and all uniting in
cherishing still more hope for the future.

SIR WILFRED LAURIER
Prime Minister of Canada (1896-1911) January 18, 1904

In many ways, the city of Windsor reflects, in microcosm, the general Canadian experience. Our first permanent settlers, after the Indians, were French, who in turn were followed by the British, and subsequently by people from the world over.

The harmonious co-existence that thrives in our city has come about through acceptance, tolerance and close communication. We relate well with one another at the local level. Unfortunately, because of the vastness of this country, and the isolation of far-flung communities, our modus operandi is ineffective on a large scale. The same type of communion just does not exist between remote locations as it does in our city.

Communities separated by two or three thousand miles have little comprehension of each other's regional problems. Maritimers, for instance, while they may sympathize to an extent, cannot fully comprehend the problems faced by people in the Prairie Provinces, just as the difficulties encountered by Maritime fishermen or pulp mill workers may be little understood by a Windsor auto worker 1,500 miles away. Sadly, the East is separated from the West, the North from the South, by much more than mere miles.

Upon reflection, it is remarkable that we have survived this long as a nation! Certainly it has been understanding that has kept us together. We almost seem to have survived despite ourselves.

Now, however, the situation has reached a stage where a conscious effort must be made to communicate with, and understand, other Canadians hitherto remote from us. And this will not be an easy task. We all continue to be absorbed in our immediate problems, and there are few ready channels for communion between distant areas.

But, if there is value and meaning in the preservation of our country, we must deliberately establish means of communion and determine to use them. As is the case between individuals, meaningful relationships between entire communities can only flourish through a constant exchange of information and ideas and a sense of neighborliness — or even kinship.

The viability of our nation hinges on our ability to recognize and encourage cultural diversity and at the same time concentrate on our common objectives.

BERT WEEKS
Mayor of Windsor, Ontario

I quailed with apprehension when a Toronto radio station recently invited me to express my feeling toward Canada in fifty seconds, as part of a series designed to encourage Canadians to think about their heritage and generally raise the national consciousness. I cowered at the thought of all the backs and hairs that could be raised by the editing and succinctness that such brevity necessitates. Whatever I said, or left unsaid, could be my undoing, especially as I am a Canadian by adoption and catharsis. I was born somewhere betwixt and between some gulches half-an-hour before sheep-shearing time in Auckland, New Zealand, and paddled to this neck of the woods in the early 1950s.

I am not known on the rialto as a tentative and retiring social sibyl, and on certain feast days (mellowed by the Niagara grape) I have been known to jabber inexhaustibly into the early hours about such illuminating trivia as choric dancing in upper and lower Oshawa or the sex life of the guppy. And now I had fifty seconds on the Marconi wireless receiver to capsulize my innermost feelings toward my foster home at the risk of:
a) Jeopardizing my reputation (sullied at the best of times)
b) Testing the last gram of patience belonging to either my dwindling group of friends or any innocent who happened to tune in.

However, undeterred by these solemn thoughts I girded my loins, scampered enthusiastically to my desk, felt tip in left hand, and with more than a little help from the Brothers Smirnoff sat with eager anticipation for an erstwhile muse to inspire me with the recall of Proust and the concise clinical detachment of Flaubert.

In truth, I was lying in ambush for any coherent thought or idea that might come along. After two hours of concentrated doodling I was still at an impasse. I got up from my semi-recumbment position, paced the living room, fortified myself with yet another beaker of the Brothers' white lightning, lurched to the balcony and watched the sun rise over a sleeping-bagged Toronto.

I am not endowed with the mental faculty of remembering and duplicating past experiences with the lucidity and authenticity of a box brownie. Certain things I remember, but they have to be extracted from my memory bank like an old molar. But that morning last summer something began to trigger in my mind's camera. Images started clicking on and off — dispersed, fragmented frames of people, places and events somersaulted down a labrynthian maze of space and time against the cyclorama of my own unique Canadian experience. Such earth-shattering incidents as the water bomb scare of 1962, and the Rosedale curry powder riots popped into my head. And the year when the taxi cab I was sharing with Kate Reid was overturned by the mobs on Binscarth Road and we were placed in custody for possessing a carton of Tootsie-Rolls and a six pack of Diet-Fresca. Memorable evenings came to mind like the party Barbara Hamilton threw for 300 of my most intimate friends at the Harbour Light and later, a formal dance under the Bloor viaduct. At this stage of the game it was evident even to me, that any systematic organization of ideas and thoughts pertinent to the upcoming broadcast could only be detrimental. I decided then and there to wing it.

I hotfooted it up to the radio station where I was ushered into the recording studio at the appointed time, determined at all cost to hide my inner misgivings. The red light came on, and the following transcript is what came out:

"Once upon a time a Maori chieftan lost his tiki (Maori good luck charm). He had searched high and low, but to no avail. One morning in his search he came across the infant Kneebone about thirteen inches long, swaddled in a feather blanket, on the outskirts of his village. Thinking the baby could have swallowed his tiki he held the mite upside down and shook it violently, encouraging the child to live.

"Raising it as his own son until the day he became fed up with it, he placed the now-adolescent brat in a canoe and ordered him to row across the great waters to Canada. This was over twenty long years ago. I became a citizen five years later and have returned on several occasions to Aotearoa (Land of the Long White Cloud, or New Zealand) for visits with the tribe, but it was not until last year that I knew where I belonged. Thomas Wolfe said "You can't go home again." You can, if you have the courage to confront emotions like disappointment, love, hate, laughter, tears, alienation — and above all have an awareness of who you are and where you belong. I do. It's a big back yard stretching from Vancouver Island to Newfoundland, and my own small playpen is in Toronto, slightly north of Davenport and certainly south of St. Clair — and that's the truth!"

TOM KNEEBONE
Actor and entertainer

In Quebec, in 1608, the state of Canada was born, and for more than 350 years the descendants of the pioneers and explorers of the 17th century have shared in the development and progress of our country. Their contribution in all areas reflects the French culture from which they originated.

As a result of the difficulties faced in other provinces in maintaining their cultural identity, French Canadians — regrouped principally in Quebec — have come to think of themselves more and more as Québécois. It is essential for our country's unity that the Québécois feel at home, accepted and respected in all provinces, and that they should have the full schooling and linguistic rights due to equal partners in the building of Canada.

A l'époque où j'étais maire de Québec, j'ai beaucoup voyagé dans toutes les provinces du Canada et j'ai constaté qu'il ne saurait y avoir d'unité nationale dans notre pays sans une affirmation permanente et réelle de nos particularités propres, de nos différences individuelles, culturelles et régionales car, à travers elles, c'est la personnalité et la liberté de chacun qui s'expriment. L'amour et l'amitié supposent le respect de l'originalité profonde des êtres chers, c'est d'ailleurs la condition essentielle de notre propre épanouissement économique, social et culturel. N'est-ce pas, en vérité, le propre de l'homme de s'ouvrir aux autres.

Only under these conditions too, will the Québécois be fully able to identify themselves as Canadians. Only when they are sure that they will be able to live and die with their French heritage, in all parts of the country, will they feel that they belong to the whole of Canada.

We must all rethink the spirit of Confederation, and base it on a respect for each founding group's identity. We must be prepared to establish a rich and healthy cultural pluralism, with no tendency toward the domination of one group by another. We Canadians must try to know each other better, to understand and to respect each other better.

By these means, whether our language is French or English, we will develop a feeling of pride in being Canadians, and we will acquire the will to work together in close collaboration to build a great country, a country as great as our common ideal.

J. GILLES LAMONTAGNE
Postmaster General

I like to think that subconscious Canada is even more important than conscious Canada and that there is growing up swiftly in this country, under the surface, the sense of a great future and of a great separate destiny . . . as Canada.

JOHN GRIERSON
Founder of National Film Board, 1946

When I was growing up in Winnipeg, I always thrilled to the singing of "O Canada." A half century later, living and working in the United States, I still remain a Canadian citizen and still thrill to the singing of the Canadian national anthem. There is a chauvinism that lies in all our hearts. But this feeling for "O Canada" and for Canada as a motherland is not predicated on two Canadas, one French and one English. It is based on one wide dominion.

I believe in the mosaic structure — a structure that can be broken into individual pieces, with each piece retaining something of its own. Translated into the Canadian mosaic, it means that we as Canadians can be broken down into ethnic, religious and geographic units. Yet all of these units come together to make for a whole — one strong, united Canada

I have no fear of the French Canadian national price. The French Canadian deserves to be proud and if he has been deprived of his share of the spoils, then let us right that wrong. If I do have a fear, it is the fear of the wedge that is being driven between the French and the English in Canada. All Canadians have a stake in the future of their country. Remember, if the problem today is Quebec, then tomorrow it is Newfoundland, perhaps the Maritimes or British Columbia — each province feeling its isolation, each concerned with its particular needs.

I have engaged in rhetoric for causes of one kind or another for a quarter of a century or more, and I can testify to the fact that it is easy to inflame passions, difficult to calm angered minds and hearts. If ever there was a time for cool rational heads to prevail, the time is now. There is no hope in harangue, no accommodation in accusation, and certainly no satisfactory answer in exodus.

MONTY HALL
Canadian T.V. Personality

We have travelled far with ourselves
and our names have lengthened;
we have carried ourselves
on our backs, like canoes
in a strange portage, over trails,
insinuating leaves
and trees dethroned like kings,
from water-route to
water-route
seeking the edge, the end,
the coastlines of this land.

GWENDOLYN MACEWEN
from "The Portage"

I believe that the challenge ahead is one that should bring Canadians together — with a new sense of purpose and commitment. Political partisanship has no place in this debate. Liberals in Ottawa, Progressive Conservatives in Ontario, New Democrats in Saskatchewan all have a duty to set aside divisions of party in search of a common unity of purpose. A Liberal but divided Canada provides no more hope than a Conservative but divided Canada. We should remember that and judge our leaders accordingly.

I am not prepared to see this country and its people, this province and my own, the West and the Maritimes ripped apart by those who would limit their hearts and minds at a time when strength and stability can be gained only through openness and understanding.

This is my land; Montreal is my metropolis as much as Toronto is yours; Québécois athletes, performers and writers are as much a part of my heritage as those of my own province.

I am not prepared to see the Canadian dream, a dream which is as much the birthright of the youngster in Trois Rivières or Rivière-du-Loup as it is the birthright of the youngster in Brampton, Chatham, or Medicine Hat, squandered, wasted and dissipated by a lack of effort and a lack of caring, or by a failure of spirit or will.

In Ontario, we place Canada first. We do so because we see in Canada the ultimate framework for the cultural, economic and political self-fulfilment of each and every citizen who shares this nation with us. That fulfilment must be multi-dimensional, balanced and fair. It must be a fulfilment that every Canadian reaches in his or her own way, shaped according to his or her own values.

The political and economic integrity of this nation has always been Ontario's major political and economic purpose.

In that we shall persist, we shall persevere, and we shall, as Canadians, succeed together.

WILLIAM C. DAVIS
Premier of Ontario

... There are expressions of *bonne entente* on both sides, but one cannot build national unity simply on the exchange of compliments. The real compliment between friends is an honest expression of views in the light of mutual understanding.

VINCENT MASSEY
Governor General of Canada (1952-59)

This is a beauty
of dissonance,
this resonance
of stony strand,
this smoky cry
curled over a black pine
like a broken
and wind-battered branch
when the wind
bends the tops of the pines
and curdles the sky
from the north.
This is the beauty
of strength
broken by strength
and still strong.

A.J.M. SMITH
from "The Lonely Land"

The Canadian concept of various people retaining and sharing their cultural heritage, while remaining united by the common bond of one strong, growing country, is nowhere better exemplified than in the Northwest Territories.

We have a mixture of Inuit, Indian, and other residents speaking two Eskimo dialects, seven Indian languages, English and French, all proud of their heritage and equally proud to be Canadians.

As in other parts of Canada, we are faced with overcoming the extreme problems of climate, transportation and communications resulting from our geography. But it is by coping with common problems that our country will be strengthened.

If the unity of Canada is threatened by the political situation in Quebec, it will certainly not be the first time we have had to unite to overcome a crisis. The threat of domination by the United States had a great deal to do with our uniting in a Confederation in 1867. Two world wars brought us together, as never before, to fight against a threat to our freedom and way of life.

I believe that the vast majority of Canadians, in all parts of our country, have a love for Canada that is deeply ingrained. It may not always be vocal or very visible, but it surfaces when needed.

I believe Canada will remain united because that is what her people want.

STUART M. HODGSON
Commissioner of the Northwest Territories

In our society we greatly value our material standard of living. When we feel threatened, one of the first questions that occurs to us is—how will we be affected economically? With the prospect of Quebec's independence becoming a reality, this is perhaps one of the questions most frequently discussed. Canadians on either side of Quebec want to know what the economic impact will be of splitting the country geographically. The frankest answer is that we do not know.

I am prepared to discuss this problem from a Maritime perspective. But, in all honesty, I wish to share my thoughts on the larger question of Quebec's relationship with the rest of Canada. I prefer not to confine my remarks entirely to the economics of the matter.

I say this because I am concerned that our tendency to measure the value of something by its economic effect may not help us to solve basic problems. For example, I am sure most of you expect to hear me condemn the independence movement in Quebec on the grounds that it is economically harmful to the Maritime region. But do we expect that such an argument would change the minds of the Québécois convinced that independence is right for them?

And what if it is found that independence will have little economic impact upon the Maritimes? Does that justify a lessening of our concern about Quebec leaving? Would Maritimers and Canadians in other regions sleep easier because we would not have to fear any material loss at the prospect of independence for Quebec? If we would draw such a conclusion, is there any wonder that we are facing a problem of national unity?

We in English Canada have shown a remarkable lack of sensibility in responding to French Canada's needs. For example, when the Québécois were concerned about assimilation and asked the government to help stem this tide by dealing with Francophones in their own language, the English media emphasized the objections of civil servants who were afraid of missing promotions. When the Prime Minister tried to make us aware of the importance of recognizing French Canada's need to protect its culture in the context of constitutional review, we tended to respond cerebrally, by emphasizing the legal and technical aspects of passing an Act through Westminster and by stressing the mechanics of repatriation. We became too defensive to think with our hearts. We tended to intellectualize the problem. To the frustration of the Québécois, we rationally asked, "What is it Quebec wants? Make us a list," we said. "Let us put these requests into concrete terms we can deal with."

I would like to say to the people of Quebec that separation may not necessarily lead you to the independence you seek. A divorce often appears as an easy solution to a troubled relationship. But a divorce often creates more difficult problems than it solves. This is true even if a relationship is being ended, not to avoid trouble, but because one of the partners wants more freedom and independence. I earnestly believe that changes can be made so that you do not have to leave the relationship to ensure that the French culture has the opportunity to healthily evolve. In fact, leaving the relationship will not automotically ensure the continued health of the French culture in North America.

If Quebec were to leave, life would still go on; we do not absolutely need Quebec to survive. But we do not want Quebec to leave, and we must find a way to convey these feelings to the Québécois.

ALEXANDER B. CAMPBELL
Premier of Prince Edward Island

We must move back:
there are too many foregrounds.

Now, clutter of twigs
across our eyes, tatter
of birds at the eye's edge; the straggle
of dead treetrunks; patch
of lichen
and in love, tangle
of limbs and fingers, the texture
of pores and lines on the skin.
vii)
An other sense tugs at us:
we have lost something,
some key to these things
which must be writings
and are locked against us
or perhaps (like a potential
mine, unknown vein
of metal in the rock)
something not lost or hidden
but just not found yet

that informs, holds together
this confusion, this largeness
and dissolving:
not above or behind
or within it, but one
with it: an

identity:
something too huge and simple
for us to see.

MARGARET ATWOOD
from "A Place: Fragments"

Rest assured, if we remain long
fragments, we shall be lost; but let us be
united, and we shall be as a rock which,
unmoved itself, flings back the waves
that may be dashed upon it by the
storm.

THOMAS D'ARCY McGEE (1825-1868)
Father of Confederation

When I think of Canada, I think of a people moulded by a harsh climate. If there is any one common bond we have as Canadians, it is the incessant struggle between man and nature — the building of the railways across the muskeg of northern Ontario and the treacherous Rockies, the building of the St. Lawrence Seaway, and the building of the oil and gas pipelines across three thousand miles of sparsely-populated land.

It is the commonality of the experience we share today with the first settlers who struggled to build a life, to build a home against nature, which gives us Canada. It is the breadth of our land, the depth of our rivers. It is the stark reality of man's lonely march toward self-fulfilment in a big, bountiful and beautiful land.

It is feelings such as this which mould us together as Canadians, which despite our ethnic, cultural and regional differences give us a sense of pride in being Canadian. A strong, national government is essential to this Canadian identity.

DAVID COLLENETTE
M.P. York East, Ontario

I know a man whose school could never teach him patriotism, but who acquired that virtue when he felt in his bones the vastness of his land, and the greatness of those who founded it.

PIERRE E. TRUDEAU
Prime Minister of Canada,
from "Exhaustion and Fulfilment: The Ascetic in a Canoe"

This is the flag of the future, but it does not dishonor the past.

LESTER B. PEARSON
Prime Minister of Canada (1963-68), House of Commons, December 15, 1964

It [Canada] brought me into the world
without a silver spoon in my mouth, but
it taught me the lesson which the
sterner laws of the North always seem
to teach its sons and daughters, that
you must look ahead, and not think only
of the passing moment; that bigness
should belong to your own life as well
as to the map of your own country.

MARY PICKFORD
from *Sunshine and Shadow*, 1955

... I am a Canadian first, last and all the time.

SIR WILFRED LAURIER
Prime Minister of Canada (1896-1911), House of Commons, February 3, 1910

Contributors

Photographers